JAPAN

CAUGHT IN TIME

JAPAN

CAUGHT IN TIME

HUGH CORTAZZI AND TERRY BENNETT

NEW YORK · WEATHERHILL · TOKYO

First edition 1995

Published by Weatherhill Inc., 420 Madison Avenue, New York, NY 10017
by special arrangement with Garnet Publishing Ltd. UK.
Copyright © 1995 Garnet Publishing Ltd
Text Copyright © 1995 Hugh Cortazzi and Terry Bennett
The right of Hugh Cortazzi and Terry Bennett to be identified as the authors of this work has
been asserted in accordance with the Copyright, Design and Patents Act, 1988.

ISBN 0 8348 0343 7

Research: Maria F. Matveeva (Keeper of the archive of the Russian Geographical Society in
St Petersburg) and Alexander Zhoukov, Senior Researcher of the Centre of Japanese Studies
of the Institute of Oriental Studies, Moscow

Reproduction of archive photographs: Svetlana Shevelchinskaya
Photographs on pages 34, 36 and 41 kindly supplied by Terry Bennett

Project management: Jackie Jones
Design: PAUL COOPER DESIGN
Reprographics: CCTS, London
Printed in Hong Kong

CONTENTS

PREFACE

The photographs in this book were collected in Japan during 1879–80 by the Russian botanist Alexander Vasilyevich Grigoryev. The prints, which have been preserved in the archives of the Russian Geographical Society in St Petersburg, have never before been published as a collection. Although prints of some of these photographs have, as Terry Bennett explains, appeared in other books, many are unique as well as outstanding examples of early photography in Japan. The photographs are undated but were for the most part taken in the 1870s.

Photography came to Japan at a very significant time in the country's history. 1868 saw the end of the Edo Period, during which Japan had been closed to almost all contacts with the West. This meant that while the European powers were dividing up large parts of the world as they vied for power and influence, in Japan life remained virtually unchanged and Japanese were largely ignorant of Western industrial and scientific developments.

Japan was almost entirely unknown to the West, and vice versa. As the following text explains, after the 1868 Meiji Restoration all this changed. From 1859 onwards foreigners were permitted to enter Japan once more. Japan in these years was just beginning the process which was to take the country from isolation and Japanese-style feudalism to the establishment of a modern industrialized state – the country had started on a fast but largely bloodless 'revolution' which would alter the whole fabric of society and government. This period coincided with the advent of photography in Japan, and the photographs of the time recorded a way of life that was fast being altered, almost beyond recognition, by the changes taking place.

This collection provides a unique 'snapshot' of Japan as it was in the early years after the country's reopening to the West. The photographs of the foreign settlements show one aspect of the new Japan. Many of the others, depicting the clothing and the activities of Japanese in town and country, give us a picture of how people lived and worked at that time. Through these photographs, which were hand-coloured at the time, we can get a much better and more accurate feel for the way in which the ordinary Japanese in the middle of the 19th century lived than we can from the artists' sketch books and the popular prints of the day, or even from the descriptive accounts of the many foreign visitors who came to Japan after the reopening of the country.

HISTORICAL BACKGROUND

BY HUGH CORTAZZI

The foreigners who came to Japan in the middle of the 19th century knew very little about the country, its history or its civilization. They thought for instance that the Shōgun, who was the titular head of the government and who was often referred to as the Taicoon *(Taikun)* was the 'Emperor' (a title only adopted for the Mikado in the latter half of the 19th century to put him on a par with the Emperors of China, Germany and Russia). Only gradually did the foreigners realize that the Mikado was, nominally at least, supreme. This was hardly surprising as few books were available about Japan and even the best, such as the two-volume history of Japan, first published in 1727–28, by Engelbert Kaempfer (who had served as doctor to the Dutch merchant colony on Dejima in the bay of Nagasaki) did not differentiate clearly between the roles of the Shōgun and the Mikado.

EARLY HISTORY

The Japanese people came from the mainland of Asia in prehistoric times; they are primarily Mongoloid but with an admixture from the indigenous tribes of the Japanese islands and from the southern part of Asia. According to Japanese mythology the first Japanese Emperor, Jimmu, established his dominion in 660 BC, but few dates before the 5th century in the Christian era are accurate. Japanese tribes from the southern island of Kyūshū gradually established themselves in the early centuries of the Christian era as the dominant power in the Kansai region (around the present cities of Osaka, Kyoto and Nara) and in the following centuries the *emishi* (literally 'barbarians') were pushed back into the northern tip of the main island of Honshū and into what is now called Hokkaidō. The few remaining pure-bred *Ainu* of Hokkaidō are probably the descendants of the *emishi*.

A wet-rice culture replaced the earlier hunting and fishing way of life over two thousand years ago and was an important element in the domination of the Kyūshū tribes, who spread rice culture through the islands of Shikoku and Honshū. Rice cultivation required relatively sophisticated use of water resources, hence co-operation between the various cultivators. Comparatively complex social organizations thus began to emerge and a form of nature worship, a primitive type of Shintō (literally the way of the gods), evolved. Yet only when meaningful contacts were established with Korea and with China and Japan began to feel and accept cultural influences from these two countries, did Japanese civilization begin to develop in any significant way.

The main elements in the civilizing process were Chinese methods of government and administration, Confucian and Buddhist thought and practices, Chinese and Korean arts, crafts and architectural forms, and Chinese language and literature. Chinese cultural influences were dominant, and by the time the capital was moved to Kyoto in 794 Japan had the appearance in many respects of being a form of Chinese state (though there was no political influence or control from the mainland). Japanese was still the language in daily use, though Chinese was employed by scholars and government officials for official documents and in the writing of poetry. (There was no written form of Japanese, so Chinese characters were adapted to represent Japanese words – this required remarkable ingenuity as Chinese is monosyllabic and tonal, while Japanese is polysyllabic and has no tones). By the 10th and 11th centuries a distinctly Japanese form of civilization had evolved, combining Chinese and Buddhist elements with indigenous ways of thought and behaviour. During these two centuries the culture and society of the court in Kyoto, then called Heiankyo, reached their high point (the highly sophisticated world of the court in the 11th century is depicted in one of the greatest novels in the world, *The Tale of Genji*, by Murasaki Shikibu).

Life in the rest of the country was, however, tough and primitive. By the 12th century the provinces came increasingly under the control of local military leaders, who developed into warlords, and at the end of that century one group, the Minamoto, defeated another major group, the Taira, in a long-drawn-out civil war; they established a military regime called the *bakufu* (literally camp government) at Kamakura, on the coast not far from the modern city of Yokohama. The Minamoto leader was appointed 'barbarian-quelling general' or, in shortened form, shōgun.

The Kamakura *bakufu* or Shogunate lasted from 1185–1333. Its power was undermined by two attempts by the Mongols, in 1274 and 1281, to invade Japan. Both failed, but weakened the regime so much that it was easily defeated by the military leader Ashikaga Takauji. In the next two centuries the Ashikaga Shogunate was nominally in control from Kyoto, but the country was wracked by almost constant civil wars as warlords fought for land and power.

CONTACT WITH THE WEST

Contacts with China had lapsed after the 9th century but were resumed from the 14th century. Despite the almost constant wars life went on and trade developed.

The first Westerners to reach Japan were the Portuguese, in the middle of the 16th century. Among the earliest to arrive was the Jesuit missionary Francis Xavier (later canonized) who reached Japan in 1549 and stayed until 1551. From this beginning the Portuguese Jesuits worked hard to promote Christianity and succeeded over the next fifty years in making significant numbers of converts, especially in Kyūshū. The Portuguese, who established a base at Maçao (off the South China coast) in about 1555, began to develop a significant trade with Japan and were granted special privileges at the port of Nagasaki.

The Ashikaga Shogunate was finally ended in 1573. The country was unified by the efforts of three successive outstanding military rulers Oda Nobunaga, Toyotomi Hideyoshi and Tokugawa Ieyasu. This was the so-called Momoyama period which may be said to have lasted from 1573–1603. During this period there was a renewal of energy and enterprise, and the arts flourished.

At first the Christian missionaries seemed to have established at least a working arrangement with Oda Nobunaga, and subsequently with Toyotomi Hideyoshi, but they aroused both the enmity of the Buddhist priests and fears that the Christian missionaries were precursors of foreign colonists. Toyotomi Hideyoshi, as he grew older, became increasingly unpredictable and began a sporadic persecution of the Christians. This was intensified after 1603, when Tokugawa Ieyasu assumed the supreme power and the Shogunate following the battle of Sekigahara.

The arrival of Dutch merchants in 1600 had meant that the Portuguese no longer had a monopoly of trade – the Dutch made no secret of their enmity towards the Portuguese and the Catholic Church. In 1613 they were joined by a group of English merchants and both groups established bases (called factories) at Hirado to the north of Nagasaki in Kyūshū. The next year, following various incidents, an edict was issued proscribing Christianity in Japan and expelling the missionaries. Although some went underground the Japanese authorities intensified the persecution of the Christians; in 1640 trade with Portugal was finally cut off, and the years of seclusion began. A small number of Dutch merchants were allowed to stay, however, but they were confined to the small, artificial island of Dejima, off Nagasaki. (The English factory at Hirado had failed and closed in 1623.) The Dutch at Dejima were thus to remain, throughout more than two hundred years of isolation, Japan's one window to the West.

The years from 1603–1868 were those of the Tokugawa Shogunate. The period is also referred to as the Edo period as the Tokugawa shōguns established their headquarters in Edo, the modern Tokyo.

During the Tokugawa, or Edo, period Japan enjoyed more than two centuries free from civil wars. Society stabilized and with the development of trade and communications a relatively prosperous merchant class emerged. Yet Tokugawa society was rigidly hierarchical, with neither flexibility nor the possibility of real social reform. The four classes were, in descending order of social standing, the samurai, the farmers, the artisans and the merchants. The farmers were, in theory, second in importance to the samurai; however, they were not allowed any freedom to move from the land, were taxed heavily to provide for the unproductive samurai, and were generally very poor. The merchants were necessary (not least to provide funds for the samurai), but they were despised and treated with contempt by the samurai. By the middle of the 19th century there had been very few moves to establish any kind of modern industry.

The country was divided into fiefs, each under the nominal control of a 'feudal' chieftain, or daimyō. The daimyō had their own samurai retainers to run the fiefs and extract taxes from the peasants. Daimyō were divided into two groups, the *fudai*, who had a special relationship with the Tokugawa and were given fiefs in strategic positions, and the *tozama* (or outer lords) who had the remaining fiefs. All had to spend part of their time in Edo, and to maintain mansions (*yashiki*) there. Whenever they returned to their fiefs they were obliged to leave their wives and children in Edo as hostages, to guarantee their loyalty to the Shōgun.

The city of Edo expanded round the castle moats and became increasingly prosperous. It and the city of Osaka were the main centres of trade and of the popular culture that developed during the 17th, 18th and first half of the 19th centuries.

Kyoto, meanwhile, where the Mikado resided and maintained an impoverished court, was something of a backwater, although its temples and sights attracted Japanese citizens who travelled there along the main highways (of which the Tōkaidō, Eastern Sea Road, is the most famous). These roads were divided into stages (there were 53 on the Tōkaidō) with inns at each stage — there was no wheeled traffic, and few bridges.

Agriculture was primitive and the food supply vulnerable to frequent natural disasters — fires, earthquakes and typhoons. The burden of taxation, especially in times of famine, caused much distress and rioting occurred from time to time. Various efforts at reform were attempted, though with limited success, largely because of the rigidity of the hierarchical structure of Japanese society.

Japan — cut off from the West by a deliberate act of policy — was unable to grasp the changes taking place in the rest of the world. A few scholars were allowed to study Western science through the medium of Dutch, but these so-called *Rangakusha* (literally 'Dutch-learning people'), although they had some limited impact on aspects of society, had no influence on government. Japanese nationalism and xenophobia were actively encouraged. At this time during the 19th century both the incompetence and the decreasing power of the regime in Edo incited the *tozama* daimyō to question the authority of the Tokugawa, and to focus on the historical role of the Mikado.

It was at this point that the Western powers began to knock on the closed doors of Japan.

THE OPENING OF JAPAN TO THE BEGINNING OF THE MEIJI ERA (1853–1868)

Although the Russians had pushed their way eastwards through Siberia and were coming into contact with Japanese outposts (see below), it fell to the Americans to force open the door to Japan. American whalers were operating in the North Pacific and wanted safe havens and supplies; these had been denied to them. The Americans, the British and the French also wanted to establish trading links with Japan, as they had already done with China.

An American fleet (the 'black ships') led by Commodore Matthew Perry arrived in waters near Edo on 8 July 1853. They sought fair treatment of shipwrecked seamen, the opening of Japanese ports, and the establishment of trade relations. The bakufu authorities were reluctant to respond, and vacillated. Perry said he would return in the following year. He did so, and an agreement was eventually concluded on 31 March 1854, providing for the immediate opening of the port of Shimoda at the tip of the Izu peninsula (which was then remote from Edo) and for the opening of Hakodate in Hokkaidō in 1855. The Americans were permitted to station a consul at Shimoda, but Perry obtained no concessions on trade. Later that year the British Admiral Sir James Stirling arrived in Nagasaki and similar arrangements were made, except that Nagasaki, rather than Shimoda, was specified as one of the two treaty ports. Agreements with the Russian Admiral Putiatin and with the Dutch followed in 1855.

These agreements were, however, unsatisfactory as they made no provision for trade. The American Consul Townsend Harris, working largely from his remote and lonely outpost at Shimoda, finally prevailed and concluded a new treaty in 1858; treaties with the British, Dutch, Russians and French followed. These treaties provided for extraterritorial rights (i.e. foreign jurisdiction over foreign residents), the appointment of diplomatic agents with the right to reside in Edo and the opening for trade in 1859 of the ports of Hakodate, Kanagawa and Nagasaki (to be followed later by the opening of other ports, in particular Hyogo near Osaka). In 1859 the Japanese authorities built a settlement at Yokohama, across the bay from Kanagawa, and in practice Yokohama became the main trading port in the 1860s. The opening of Hyogo, which later became the port of Kobe, was

delayed until 1868. The main exports of the treaty ports were tea and raw silk. The British merchants were soon the dominant community in Yokohama. Nagasaki retained its importance as a trading post until 1868 as it was the main base for supplies to the Western fiefs. Hakodate was remote and little trade developed there in these years. It was of greater importance to the Russians than to the other powers. In these early days the treaty ports, in particular Yokohama, were insecure, rough and tough places for the merchant adventurers

'Bund', the quay in the European quarter of Yokohama

A street in the Japanese part of Yokohama

from the treaty countries, with frequent murderous attacks on foreigners and many health hazards.

The impotence and vacillation of the *bakufu* aroused the ire of the foreign representatives, as well as of the daimyō and samurai who resented Tokugawa dominion. They had been educated to resent and despise the 'red-headed barbarians' and regarded the foreigners as fair game. The battle cry of the xenophobes was '*Sonnō Jōi*' ('Revere the Emperor and expel the barbarians').

Treaty Point, Yokohama

The *bakufu* proved unable to guard properly even the legations and diplomats stationed in Edo. Garrisons, primarily British and French, had to be brought in to protect the foreigners after there had been many dangerous incidents. One of the most serious was the murder in 1862 at Namamugi, on the Tōkaidō (Eastern Sea Road) near Yokohama, of a British merchant from Shanghai; he had been riding with two companions when they had encountered the train of the daimyō of Satsuma (now Kagoshima prefecture in southern Kyūshū). The British were able to obtain satisfaction from neither the *bakufu* nor the fief. So in 1863 a British fleet was sent to Kagoshima; the town was bombarded and much of it burnt down. The Satsuma forces inflicted casualties on the British fleet and did not acknowledge their defeat, but they recognized that the Japanese were in no position to withstand a prolonged assault from well-trained and armed Western forces. Japan had had firearms since their introduction by the Portuguese in the 16th century, but possessed practically no modern cannon or other armaments. The Satsuma authorities now bought arms and ships through the port of Nagasaki, in particular via a Scottish merchant, Thomas Glover, and began to make overtures of friendship towards the British.

The straits of Shimonoseki, between the main island of Honshū and the southern island of Kyūshū, became the next focus of trouble. The straits were controlled by the Chōshū clan which, motivated by a combination of anti-foreign feeling and a determination to embarrass the *bakufu*, fired on vessels attempting to pass through the straits, then closed the straits to foreign shipping. Foreign representatives, under the leadership of Sir Rutherford Alcock, the British Minister, responded by launching an attack on Chōshū batteries in 1864. These were spiked and the Chōshū authorities forced to accept the reopening of the straits.

The foreigners, recognizing the impotence of the *bakufu*, wanted the court in Kyoto to accept the treaties. The Mikado was, however, becoming increasingly the puppet of the *tozama* daimyō: he was being used to force the submission of the *bakufu*, who were unable to carry out the court demand that the hated foreigners should be expelled. The *bakufu* tried – and failed – to deal effectively with Chōshū, which made up its quarrels with Satsuma. Both fiefs came increasingly under the control of powerful and intelligent younger samurai some of whom, through the good offices of Thomas Glover, had been smuggled out to Britain to study.

In 1867 both the Mikado and the Shōgun died. The new Mikado, Mutsuhito – known by his reign name of Meiji – was a boy. The new Shōgun however, Tokugawa Keiki, was an experienced politician who could see the need for radical change. In November 1867 Keiki submitted his resignation as Shōgun, but his followers wanted to hang on to their power and their fiefs; civil war broke out in January 1868. The Tokugawa forces were defeated at Toba-Fushimi on the outskirts of Kyoto, Osaka castle was set on fire and Keiki forced to escape to Edo. 'Imperial' forces consisting of troops from the *tozama* fiefs, in particular Satsuma and Chōshū, led largely by the Satsuma general Saigo Takamori, were soon in control of Edo and the main centres of the country. Civil war continued, however, in central and northern Japan until the late autumn of 1868 and in Hokkaidō (where rebel forces held out at Hakodate) until early 1869.

The port of Hyogo (Kobe) was opened on 1 January 1868. The British, particularly Ernest Satow of the British Legation, had established good relations with the younger samurai from Satsuma and Chōshū who were to form the Satchō oligarchy in Meiji Japan. Sir Harry Parkes, the fiery British Minister, had been ordered to maintain neutrality in the Japanese civil war but was nevertheless contemptuous of the *bakufu*, whom he found untrustworthy and feeble. (Parkes had also quarrelled with his French colleague, Leon Roches, who had supported the *bakufu* with military and naval missions.) The new regime, which carried out what was termed the 'Meiji Restoration' was recognized by the foreign governments. A revolution had begun.

THE MEIJI ERA (1868–1912)

The new government was ostensibly a coalition between two groups: the court nobles and the leaders of the clans who had led the struggle against the Tokugawa. Yet the real power lay with a number of younger samurai primarily, although not exclusively, from Satsuma and Chōshū. They filled most of the key junior posts and came to dominate the bureaucracy that developed to administer the government. The slogan representing their aims was 'fukoku kyōhei' (a rich country and a strong army). Their ambition for Japan was initially for the ending of the 'unequal' treaties of 1858, including extraterritoriality, and subsequently for equality with the leading world powers.

In 1868 this was a distant prospect, but the young samurai were able and determined. They saw that the 'feudal' system operating in Japan – which involved penal taxation of the peasantry to support an unproductive samurai class – was incompatible with a modern state. The revenue had to be used to develop the country. Moreover the fiefs, with their strong local interests, were the antithesis of the strong, centralized state the young samurai believed necessary in order to achieve their aims. The new government accordingly moved quickly to dismantle the old system. The fiefs were abolished and replaced by prefectures. The samurai were pensioned off on terms very unfavourable to the pensioners; they were soon forbidden even to wear the traditional two swords which had marked them off from the commoner. To add insult to injury the new regime instituted a system of universal conscription that brought members of the peasantry into the new army. A few industrial enterprises had been established in the final decades of the Edo period by the Tokugawa and by some of the fiefs; these were now encouraged by the new regime and, in the absence of a class of middle-class entrepreneurs, were funded and organized from the centre in a form of state capitalism (although they were later privatized). Shintō was adapted to form a state religion and was used to support the role of the Mikado, both as 'high priest' and as a national unifying symbol. Meanwhile Buddhist temples, which had previously existed alongside and in co-operation with

Shintō shrines, were harshly treated and in some places destroyed. The Tokugawa prohibition on Christianity was maintained until foreign pressures forced a modification of the anti-Christian edicts.

The 1870s in Japan were a period of revolutionary change: for some of the less enlightened samurai the changes were too many and too fast. Samurai chauvinism found some outlet in an expedition against Formosa (Taiwan), but such adventures were insufficient to mop up samurai discontent. Following troubles in northern Kyūshū samurai resentment in the southern fief of Satsuma boiled over, in 1877, in what was called the *Seinan Sensō* (South-West war) or the Satsuma rebellion. This was led by Saigo Takamori, who had played such an influential part in the Meiji Restoration of 1868. The rebels besieged the castle of Kumamoto in Kyūshū, but were repulsed by forces that included conscripts. They were finally defeated and Saigo Takamori committed suicide. Later he was rehabilitated and he is still one of Japan's tragic heroes.

After the rebellion the unity of the country and of 'imperial rule' were assured. The development of the Japanese economy and polity in the next decades inevitably had its ups and downs, but by the end of the century Japan had become a world power. A constitution, even if an autocratic one, was granted in 1889 and parliamentary institutions operated from 1890. The 'unequal' treaties were amended in 1894 and in 1899 new arrangements came into force. During the Sino-Japanese war of 1894–95 Japan surprised most Western observers by defeating Chinese forces, but Japanese pride was badly dented by the triple intervention (by Russia, France and Germany) which denied the Japanese some of the spoils in China which they regarded as their due. Russo-Japanese rivalry in North-East Asia, especially Korea, provided the background to the Anglo-Japanese alliance of 1902 and to the Russo-Japanese war of 1904–5. Japanese victories, including the defeat of the Russian navy at the battle of the Japan Sea (also called the battle of Tsushima), increased Japanese self-confidence.

ECONOMIC DEVELOPMENT

At the beginning of the Meiji period Japan's economy was almost totally dependent on agriculture, centred on the production of wet rice. Agricultural methods were still primitive and the harvest at the mercy of the weather. Rivers were liable to flooding, and natural disasters were frequent. Farming was highly labour intensive; there was no modern machinery and the peasants, who had provided almost the entire revenue in 'feudal' times, were still the main source of revenue. The life of the Japanese peasant remained very hard.

The government had limited resources for economic development, though industries were gradually developed. Progress was made relatively early in textiles. Initially the Japanese had to rely on imports of ships and steel, but by the end of the century basic industries had been developed (including the production of armaments) even if these were still behind those in Europe. The treaty ports, especially Yokohama and Kobe, played a significant role in Japanese economic development in the latter part of the 19th century.

In the treaty ports a foreign society developed which was to a very large extent cut off by the treaties from Japan proper, which the inhabitants of the settlements rather quaintly called 'the interior'. The foreigners had their own communities and did not mingle with the Japanese. They maintained their own separate way of life with Western-style clubs, sports, houses, hotels, food, drink and amusements. Foreigners were not wholly cut off from contacts with Japan, however. Although they had to get special passports to travel outside the treaty ports, as the years went by and Japan became more prosperous the restrictions were eased. The first railway from Yokohama to Tokyo was opened in 1872, and between Kobe and Kyoto, via Osaka, in 1876. The first lines were built and initially run by British railway engineers. They were just some of the foreign expert employees, known as *o-yatoi gaijin*, who were employed by the new government in their efforts to speed up the development of the country. Many of these government employees were able and dedicated men (although others were little more than ignorant charlatans).

The Japanese leaders were, however, determined from the beginning that Japan's dependence on foreign help should be as brief as possible. Foreign teachers were employed, partly to teach English but also to instruct in technical and other subjects. Japanese were sent abroad in large numbers to study Western technology and know-how so that they would be able to replace foreign experts.

SOME ASPECTS OF LIFE IN JAPAN IN THE 1870s

The rigid class structure, which divided the people into the four classes of samurai, farmers, merchants and artisans, was an anachronism which was ended in 1869. Conscription, introduced in 1872, undermined the position of the samurai – the final blow to their privileges came with abolition (in 1876) of their right to wear two swords, as mentioned earlier. Many of the samurai, in particular, found it difficult to adapt to their loss of role and of privileges. The younger and more sensible samurai went into the civil service or into business, but it was not easy, even for the wise among them, to recognize that they were no longer in a position to enforce obedience from 'the lower orders'. The nostalgia of the samurai for the past can be seen in such photographs as those showing archery practice (p. 94).

The farmers, although theoretically emancipated, continued to live a life of hard drudgery. The government's main source of revenue was the land tax, which bore as heavily on the farmers as had the old imposts of the fiefs. Farming methods remained primitive, without mechanization. Harvests were still subject to the vagaries of the climate and were often affected by natural disasters including typhoons and earthquakes. Many landlords behaved harshly towards their tenants, who in many cases fell into the clutches of moneylenders. Much needed to be done to build embankments and improve the supply of water to the paddies; crops needed to be improved and new fertilizers introduced in place of the human excrement used hitherto. In fact it was not until the end of the Second World War that the lot of the peasant farmers was significantly improved.

Although great efforts were made to adopt Western customs as quickly as possible, if only to try to achieve the intense Japanese wish to do away with the 'unequal' treaties, the changes in the early decades after the Restoration were largely confined to a small minority in the treaty ports and in the capital.

Japanese in all walks of life still largely wore Japanese clothing. Japanese women in formal dress wore a kimono with a sash and had their hair carefully put up. One of the most popular styles was the *ichōgaeshi*, or butterfly style. Formal dress for men was *haori* and *hakama* – a form of coat and skirt. Up to the Restoration in 1868 most Japanese men had the front parts of their heads shaved with the back hair done up in a topknot, but in 1871 a government order (the *dampatsurei*) encouraged all males to cut off their topknots. Footwear was primitive, however: most wore a form of clog (*geta*) or a type of straw sandal (*zori* or *waraji*).

Japanese houses were simple: the main room would have a floor of *tatami* (rush mats) and an alcove (the *tokonoma*) where there would probably be a hanging scroll (either a picture or a piece of calligraphy) and perhaps a vase of flowers. The sliding panels would be of paper. Such heating as there was consisted of small boxes or pots (*hibachi*) containing ash with a small amount of charcoal burning in the centre. Lighting was provided by oil lamps and candles. (The Japanese began to manufacture kerosene lamps in 1872.)

The same room was used for living and for sleeping. and the only piece of furniture would probably be a chest for clothing. When the time for sleep came Japanese mattresses/coverlets (*futon*) were produced and laid on the mats. 'Pillows' (*makura*) were hard and small (in order to preserve the hair style wooden pillows were in common use). Japanese invariably took off their shoes before stepping up on to the polished wood of a house entrance (*genkan*) or stepping on to *tatami*. Much Japanese life went on in the kitchen, where a kettle would be kept on the boil, suspended over a charcoal fire. The kitchen would have in part an earthen floor with a simple sink. Privies were primitive structures off one corner of the house. Nightsoil was collected in barrels for use on farms. Only the very rich had their own bathrooms. Most people used the public baths. (In those days mixed bathing was common although under Western influence the sexes were increasingly segregated.) The bath house was an important centre of social life and gossip. Japanese would wash themselves outside the bath, then get into a communal bath to soak and relax in the hot water and to chat with their neighbours.

Food still followed the old patterns. Rice was the staple dish, though in many poorer families millet and other grains provided a substitute. Japanese vegetables and pickles supplemented the staple food and protein was obtained from limited amounts of fish and from soya bean products. The main drink was Japanese green tea. Sake (Japanese rice wine) was drunk mainly by men and at parties where drunkenness was not only permitted but encouraged. The poorer labourers also drank shōchū, a spirit which in Kyūshū was made from sweet potatoes but which can be made from grains. Meat was practically never eaten until Western influence began to be felt, as Buddhism forbade the taking of life and Buddhist monks were supposed to live on a vegetarian diet. Fish was, however, permitted as the fish was not considered to be killed – rather, it died on coming out of the water! Some birds were eaten, especially by hunters who also killed wild boar. The euphemism for wild boar in Japan in the Edo period was 'mountain whale' (yama kujira). Some fruit was consumed but was of poor quality, since Japanese fruit had not yet been improved by modern methods of cultivation. Standards of nutrition were accordingly low.

Pastimes were few. Shōgi (Japanese chess) and go (Japanese chequers) were played. Some Japanese males still practised archery. Children enjoyed battledore and shuttlecock as well as kite-flying.

The Japanese theatre was also popular, and performances of kabuki (traditional Japanese dramas) took place regularly, often lasting all day. Theatres had quite advanced stage machinery. The audience generally sat on the floor of boxes. Sumo (Japanese style wrestling) was also a popular sport watched by many enthusiasts.

Brothels were officially permitted and the Yoshiwara was a recognized place for sex and assignations. Many of the girls operating there had been sold into prostitution by indigent families. Geisha (high-class courtesans) who were not common prostitutes, provided amusement at parties with their dancing, singing and playing on the *samisen* (a three stringed-instrument similar to a guitar).

Japanese consumer products were few and simple. The old crafts had hardly begun to change.

Most Japanese shops were primitive affairs with open fronts – the customer would be served while sitting on a verandah, where he might be given a cup of tea and smoke a pipe (Japanese pipes had very small bowls and would only give two or three puffs at most).

Transport was mainly on foot or on horseback. Some trains were running by the late 1870s, but few Japanese roads had yet been made suitable for wheeled traffic, other than of a very primitive character. The rickshaw (*jinrikisha*, meaning man-power-vehicle) was said to have been invented by an American missionary called Goble. It only came into common use in the 1870s. It could be used on primitive paths and provided work for increasing numbers of poor peasants, but pulling a rickshaw was punishing work and life expectancy among rickshaw men was particularly low. By the end of the 1870s the rickshaw had largely replaced the palanquin (*norimono*) or chair (*kago*) carried by porters and used primarily by the wealthy.

Life expectancy was generally low in those days. Medicine was still provided primarily by practitioners of Chinese medicine (*kampō*). While Chinese herbal remedies and such treatments as acupuncture brought relief to many, Chinese medicine was unable to cope with the infectious diseases and injuries which were commonplace in Japan in the 1870s, and although Western medicine was being developed, few practitioners had been trained by this time.

Japanese religious life, such as it was, continued much as before, although the forced separation of Shintō and Buddhism by the authorities led to Buddhist temples being damaged and in some cases destroyed. Japanese generally did not see why they could not continue to be adherents of both religions. Both Buddhist temples and Shintō shrines had their own festivals and traditional practices, and it was not thought incompatible to attend ceremonies at both temples and shrines. Shintō 'gods' (*kami*) were often identified with Buddhist bodhisattvas, and it is still possible today to find Shintō shrines within the precincts of Japanese Buddhist temples. Shintō shrines were distinguished from Buddhist temples not only by their differing styles of architecture but also by the fact that shrines were approached through *torii*, a form of simple gateway or arch.

As nowadays Japanese would take their children to be blessed at the local shrine which they would visit at New Year and on festival days. They would also be married at a shrine, in a Shintō ceremony. But most people would at least go to their Buddhist temple to visit the tombs of their ancestors and would expect to have a Buddhist funeral if only in the hope or belief that upon death they would become a Buddha.

Shintō, as practised in Japan in those days, had little or no ethical teaching. The main emphasis was on nature worship and ritual purity, but Shintō was beginning to be used to inculcate loyalty to the state and to the Emperor in particular. Buddhist ethics, especially the emphasis on resignation and compassion, were more important, but Japanese ethical beliefs were still primarily Confucian. In Japan unswerving loyalty was the prime virtue, although filial piety was also regarded as important.

In the 1870s the bans on Christianity were lifted but the authorities remained suspicious of Christian missionary activity and missionaries found it difficult to make much headway.

RUSSIA AND JAPAN

The compiler of the albums from which these photographs are taken was a Russian geographer-explorer, therefore the relationship between Russia and Japan in this period is worthy of a note. As Russia, from the time of Peter the Great in the late 17th and early 18th centuries, slowly expanded into Siberia, Russian explorers and officials started to come into contact with Japanese and *Ainu* people in the Kurile Islands. Japanese ships blown off course also reached Russian occupied land. The

Japanese authorities were, however, determined to maintain their country's seclusion and adamantly refused to have anything to do with any foreigners. They were even reluctant, for fear of contamination, to take back their own nationals who had been shipwrecked.

The first Japanese seaman picked up by Russians in the neighbourhood of Kamchatka was a man called Dembei who had sailed in a fleet of ships carrying products from Osaka to Edo and been blown off course in a typhoon in 1695. Dembei came into Russian hands in 1697 and eventually reached St Petersburg. He was received in 1702 by the Tsar, Peter the Great, who commanded that he be taught Russian so that in his turn he could teach Japanese to Russians. Japanese studies in Russia were formally instituted at the St Petersburg Academy of Sciences in 1736.

The first Russian ships to explore the Kurile Islands and to view the coast of Honshū were commanded by Martin Petrovich Spanberg in 1737–38. Various adventurers, including the famous Count Benyovsky, probed further, but it was not until the latter part of the 18th century and the beginning of the 19th century that serious moves were made to develop relations with Japan. Even then there was no consistency in Russian efforts and years passed between one contact and the next.

In 1787 a Japanese seaman from Wakamatsu, named Kodayu, with some fellow seamen reached Kamchatka. At Irkutsk Kodayu aroused the interest of Eric Laxman, a Finnish-born Professor of Natural Sciences at the St Petersburg Academy. Laxman proposed an expedition to return the castaways. This proposal was approved by the Tsarina, Catherine the Great, who in 1791 received Kodayu and his colleagues. After making contact with Japanese officials in the southern Kurile Islands Laxman reached Nemuro (Hokkaidō) in October 1792. They were allowed to winter there while the authorities from the Matsumae fief tried to work out with the government in Edo how to respond. Eventually, after attempts had been made to persuade the Russians to travel to Matsumae by land, Laxman was allowed to sail to Hakodate. From there he and his party were taken on to Matsumae where Laxman was eventually induced to hand over the castaways and was given a letter permitting a visit to Nagasaki – but this said nothing about trade or further contacts which the Russians sought.

It was not until 1803 that the Russians followed up. Nikolai Petrovich Rezanov was appointed as envoy to negotiate with the Japanese at Nagasaki. He quarrelled with Adam Johann von Krusenstern, who was appointed to command the Russian ships and consequently the expedition was a distinctly unhappy one. Rezanov found the Japanese authorities in Nagasaki thoroughly unhelpful and his patience was tried to the limit. He did not resort to force during the negotiations but he determined on revenge.

The subsequent depradations on Japanese in the northern territories by the Russians Khvostov and Davydov may not have been properly authorized, but they aroused Japanese ire and set off a major debate in Edo about how the government should in future react to Russian incursions. Hokkaidō and the Kuriles had hitherto been neglected and not even adequately surveyed, but surveys were now carried out and defences strengthened.

In the summer of 1811 the Russian sloop *Diana*, under the command of Lieutenant Commander Vasilii Golovnin, received orders to survey the southern Kurile Islands. At the island of Etorofu Golovnin encountered Japanese officials and after various contacts was engaged in conversations on shore when he and his companions were trapped and arrested. Golovnin and his party were taken to Matsumae and imprisoned. Golovnin's long incarceration and his eventual release through the efforts of Petr Ivanovich Rikord, who, with the help of a Japanese merchant Takadaya, took over command of the *Diana*, make a fascinating story. Rikord had to make it clear that the depradations of Khvostov and Davidov were not authorized and were regretted by the Russian authorities, but they remained a reminder to the Japanese of potential dangers threatening them from the north.

Russian efforts to open Japan were resumed in 1852, when the Russians sent Admiral Evfimii Vasilevich Putiatin in the frigate *Pallada*, together with the frigate *Vostok*, to Japan. Talks began at Nagasaki in September 1853; yet it was only on

7 February 1855 that an agreement was concluded at Shimoda, where the American Consul Townsend Harris had taken up his post. In the meantime the *Diana* had been wrecked in a tidal wave in December 1853 and the Russian seamen had had to be accommodated on shore. The Russian position was complicated by the outbreak of the Crimean War, which meant that British and French ships were on the look-out for Russian men-of-war. A very readable account of the voyage of the *Pallada* was made by the famous Russian author Goncharov.

The treaty of 1855 did not provide for the development of trade relations. These were covered by the Russo-Japanese treaty which was concluded by Putiatin and Japanese plenipotentiaries at Edo on 19 August 1858.

The first foreigners to be assassinated in Yokohama (against the background of anti-foreign sentiment) were a Russian officer and seaman in August 1859, soon after the opening of the port. On the whole, Russian behaviour in the treaty ports seems to have compared favourably with that of nationals from some of the other treaty countries. Nevertheless Russian activities in Sakhalin and in Tsushima at this time had given the Japanese grounds for concern about Russian intentions. The British too were highly suspicious of Russian motives and kept a close watch on Russian activities. In the circumstances prevailing in Japan in the 1860s and 1870s the Russians found the Americans more sympathetic.

Hakodate was more important as a treaty port for the Russians than for any of the other powers. However, trade with Russia developed slowly. One reason for this was the economic backwardness of Russian territories in the Far East.

The first representative of the Russian Orthodox Church to reach Japan was a Russian priest who arrived in Hakodate in 1858 with the first Russian consul. His successor, the monk Nikolai, was however the founder and leading light in the Orthodox Church in Japan in the Meiji period. (Even today the Orthodox Church in Tokyo situated in Kanda is called the Nikolai Cathedral.)

Much time and effort had to be devoted in these early years to determining the frontiers between Russian possessions in the Far East and Japan's northern territories.

The American scholar George Alexander Lensen, in his careful and detailed study of Russo-Japanese relations from 1697–1875 entitled *The Russian Push toward Japan* (Octagon Books, New York 1971), concludes (page 469): 'It is possible that Russia could have opened Japan at an earlier date, had she acted with greater energy and persistence. The reluctance of the tsarist government to exert military pressure encouraged the Shogunate in its policy of deferment. Yet when relations were established at last, they were established without force . . . Japanese interest in Russia was total, constant, occasionally verging on hysteria, and shaped by an overestimation of actual Russian interest in Japan.'

THE COMPILER OF THE ORIGINAL ALBUMS OF PHOTOGRAPHS

Alexander Vasilyevich Grigoryev was born in St Petersburg in 1848. He studied botany at the University of St Petersburg, graduating in 1870. In 1878 he was elected a Member of the Imperial Russian Geographical Society, where he worked until his death in 1908. In 1879 Grigoryev was sent by the Society on an expedition to help Baron Nils A. E. Nordenskjold, a Swedish traveller who had been making a voyage by the north-eastern route from the Atlantic to the Pacific and had been compelled to winter off the Siberian coast. The rescuers were to follow Nordenskjold's route in the opposite direction. The expedition, which started on 1 May 1879, reached Yokohama on 15 July. Here Grigoryev met Nordenskjold, who had successfully completed his mission. Grigoryev's expedition continued its voyage but was shipwrecked off the coast of Hokkaidō. Grigoryev, trying to derive some benefit from this misfortune, devoted approximately a year to the study of Japan. He collected important data about the language and everyday life of the *Ainu* in Hokkaidō and studied the physical geography of Japan's northern island.

Grigoryev brought back to Russia a large quantity of scientific material as well as the albums of photographs, of which a selection is included in this book.

SUGGESTIONS FOR FURTHER READING.

Anyone interested in the early history of Russo-Japanese relations should look out for the works of George Alexander Lensen especially his book cited above, *The Russian Push toward Japan*.

For general history of Japan and its culture there is *The Japanese Achievement* by Sir Hugh Cortazzi, published in 1991 by Sidgwick and Jackson. Alternatives include works by Sir George Sansom, including *Japan, a Short Cultural History* (Cresset Press, London, 1946) and *The Western World and Japan* (Cresset Press, London 1950).

A good introduction to modern Japanese history is W. G. Beasley's *The Rise of Modern Japan* (Tuttle, Tokyo, 1990).

Sir Hugh Cortazzi's *Victorians in Japan: In and Around the Treaty Ports* (Athlone, London, 1987) contains many descriptions of Japan in the early Meiji period by foreign residents and visitors. Amusing accounts are also contained in Pat Barr's two books *The Coming of the Barbarians* and *The Deer-cry Pavilion* published by Macmillan in the United Kingdom in 1967 and 1968.

THE HISTORY OF PHOTOGRAPHY IN JAPAN

BY TERRY BENNETT

I was first drawn to Japanese photography, many years ago, on seeing an album of fifty beautifully coloured early images. I thought at first, due to their stunning freshness, that these were modern coloured photographs. I had no idea that this art form existed. It turned out that, as the photographs in this book demonstrate, hand colouring of images is typical of early photography from Japan, an art in its own right.

Photography in Japan has a distinctive history. In the early days, it was much influenced by the work of certain European photographers who travelled there, established photographic studios, and set about recording every kind of detail of Japanese life. Prints of many such photographs were collected and brought to the West, and are sought after by collectors to this day.

The photographs published here all come from the collection assembled by the Russian botanist Alexander Vasilyevich Grigoryev, whose travels took him to Japan in 1879. Copies of some have appeared in other books, but many have not and are outstanding examples of early photography in Japan. The photographs were for the most part taken in the 1870s.

THE DEVELOPMENT OF PHOTOGRAPHY; ITS INTRODUCTION TO JAPAN

It is generally held that photography was invented by the Frenchman, Louis Daguerre, and made public by him in 1839. In fact he was not the inventor but he did perfect, and make practical use of, Joseph Niepce's photographic processes. (Niepce was also a Frenchman and had produced the first photograph that can be dated in 1826. Prior to that the Englishman, Tom Wedgwood, a son of the famous potter Josiah Wedgwood, had been experimenting since 1796 in trying to obtain a photographic image of botanical specimens with the use of sensitized silver salts. Around 1800 he actually produced images but could not make them permanent. In 1802 he despaired of making progress and published his results.) Daguerre, in 1839, demonstrated that an individual picture, a positive, could be produced using an appropriate camera. However, each photograph was unique and could not be replicated since there was no negative image from which to make multiple copies. The negative-positive principle was the invention of an Englishman, Henry Fox Talbot, who published his results in the same year, 1839. But it was Daguerre who caught the world's imagination, and then improvements and refinements by others proceeded at break-neck speed.

Japan would have been oblivious to this momentous event since, as Hugh Cortazzi explains in his introduction, the country was in a period of isolation. True, a few scholars could have had access to information about photography through the Dutch traders who were virtually imprisoned on the artificial island of Dejima at Nagasaki. But it is unlikely that much notice was taken and Japan continued to be cocooned in its isolated slumber.

At this point in the history of Japan's isolation, a number of feudal lords, daimyō, were anxious to loosen, if not break, the iron grip of the ruling Tokugawa dynasty, headed by the Shōgun and based in Edo (Tokyo). These daimyō saw the importation of knowledge and machinery from the West as extremely beneficial to their local economies; that they were able to do this, almost certainly against the wishes of the Shōgun, illustrates very well the gradual weakening of the Tokugawa stranglehold which had effectively been in place since 1600. Groups of students, sponsored by their 'clans', were actively studying Western medicine, science and literature. Imports of machinery and weapons were gradually on the increase.

The first camera was believed to have come to Japan in 1841, via Dejima and a wealthy Nagasaki merchant, Shinnojo Ueno (1790–1851). However, according to the Japanese photo-historian, Professor Takesi Ozawa (1) the camera was mistakenly not unloaded from the ship and was returned to Holland, so Ueno didn't get his camera until 1848. Accordingly, photography was introduced to Japan nine years after Daguerre's momentous announcement to the world and five years before the American fleet under Commodore Perry shattered Japan's isolationist policy.

EARLY EXPERIMENTS

The enterprising Ueno was a man of many talents; he was a clock-maker, gunnery-expert, artist and one of the pioneer promoters of Western science in Japan. (One of his sons, Hikoma Ueno, would become, with Renjo Shimooka, one of the first professional Japanese photographers.) The enlightened and powerful Shimazu Nariakira, leader of the Satsuma Clan based in southern Kyūshū, acquired a camera from Shinnojo Ueno in 1849 and started to experiment with it. Photographic supplies would, of course, have been extremely difficult to obtain and prohibitively expensive, and in feudal Japanese society at this time, only daimyō, like Shimazu, could contemplate such an exercise. Although some success was achieved, the results were unsatisfactory — largely because the camera was faulty. In fact the earliest surviving photograph by a Japanese was a daguerreotype portrait of Shimazu taken in 1857 by one Shiro Ichiki.

The earliest surviving collodian (wet plate) photograph taken in Japan was in 1858. The title was 'Three Princesses' and this image of three women was taken by Shimazu Nariakira and is kept in the Shimazu family museum at Kagoshima.

FIRST PHOTOGRAPHS IN JAPAN

For earlier surviving images we have to join the American photographer attached to Commodore Perry's 1852–54 expedition to Japan, Eliphalet Brown Junior (1816–86).

During this voyage he took many daguerreotypes; a number of these are illustrated in lithographic form in the standard and official book of the expedition, edited by Hawks (2). Four of the original photographs have been discovered, three of which are in museums in Japan. These 1853–54 photographs are the earliest dated images of Japan. (The rest were apparently lost when a fire in the United States destroyed the building they were kept in, shortly after publication of the book.)

In 1854, shortly after Perry and his warships left Japan, a Russian ship arrived with the photographer Captain Aleksander Mozhaiskii on board. He took a number of daguerreotypes, at least one of which has survived and is in the Gyokusenji temple in Shimoda, Japan. It is significant that no other known images of Japan pre-date 1860 — 21 years after the effective introduction of photography in the West!

WESTERN PHOTOGRAPHERS IN JAPAN

Why do no photographs of Japan taken by Westerners during the period 1854–59 exist? One of the concessions Perry obtained from the reluctant Japanese was the right for an American consul, Townsend Harris, to reside in Japan. Harris, with his assistant Henry Heusken (who would be murdered by a Japanese assassin in 1861), arrived in 1856. These were the only 19th-century Westerners permitted to live in Japan. This situation continued until July 1859 when later treaties permitted foreign residence at the treaty ports of Yokohama, Nagasaki and Hakodate.

There is the strange, but un substantiated, story of an un-named Norwegian who worked with the Dutch at Dejima in 1857. According to his lengthy narrative he took a camera with him and a Nagasaki merchant became interested in this. The Norwegian is said to have disguised himself as a Japanese and to have travelled in the locality of Nagasaki, with the merchant, taking a number of photographs. This story appeared in the *Photographic News* in a long, serialized format from October 1859–February 1860 (3). Japanese scholars do not believe this story (4), convincing as it may be in parts, and have pointed out some descriptive mistakes made by the author. Penalties for transgressions of Japanese law at the time were severe: the Japanese merchant would have been taking incredible risks and, if caught, would almost certainly have been sentenced to death. At any rate, the author's anonymity and the non-appearance of the promised photographs lead to the conclusion that this particular story, while romantic and inventive, is untrue. The only room for doubt is that, in his narrative, the Norwegian makes it clear that he has changed the names of the people and places in order to protect those involved.

Rather more frustrating is that no photographs of Japan appear to have survived from Lord Elgin's 1858 expedition. We know that the official photographer of the voyage, the Hon. William Nassau Jocelyn, took numerous wet-plate photographs since Elgin's secretary, Oliphant, mentions this in the preface to his famous book. Furthermore, Jocelyn makes several references to his own photography in his private journal which is held by the Yokohama Archives of History Museum (5).

I have no doubt that numerous photographs were taken in Japan in 1859 – the year the country was officially opened to foreigners. In fact an American resident of Yokohama, O. E. Freeman, was described as the first to open a photographic business in the port (6, 7). However, none of these photographs has yet been discovered, or at any rate attributed to this period.

Negretti & Zambra, an enterprising London photographic firm, commissioned a series of photographs of Japan (they would appear to have been taken in 1860). These were published in stereograph form in 1861, and were extremely popular. Some also appear, as original tipped-in stereos, in the exceptionally rare book by T. C. Westfield, *The Japanese, Their Manners and Their Customs* (8). Some uncertainty exists, in my mind, as to the photographer(s) of this series. They have always previously been attributed to A. A. J. Gower, a British consular official and amateur photographer (9), yet it seems more likely that they are the work of either or both the professional photographers Rossier (French) and W. B. Woodbury (English). Rossier was known as a contributor to Negretti & Zambra; he was definitely photographing in Nagasaki in 1859–60. Woodbury was also doing work for Negretti & Zambra in Java and is known to have travelled in both China and Japan (10).

The next dated photographs of Japan are by the Englishman, William Saunders, who took a number during a three-month stay from August 1862: later he settled in Shanghai, and became famous for his work in early Chinese photography (11).

The next photographer of any note to arrive, in 1863, was Charles Parker, who stayed in Japan until about 1868 (12). Unfortunately, and rather surprisingly, only a handful of Parker's *carte-de-visite* photographs, positively identified from his studio stamp appearing on the reverse, survive. Yet he must have been quite prolific, judging by the numerous advertisements for his studio that appeared in Yokohama newspapers at that time.

In the same year, 1863 (13), the already famous Italian photographer, Felice Beato, known for his exceptional work in photographing the Crimean War (1855), the Indian Mutiny (1858), and the Anglo-French military expedition to China (1860), took up residence in Yokohama. He was destined to stay for the next 21 years. Beato's work in Japan is well documented, but his place and date of birth are unknown, as is his date of death (best estimates are that he was born in Venice or Constantinople in 1825 and died in Burma in 1908 (13–19)).

Beato's Japanese portrait and landscape work are both highly acclaimed and a significant amount of his work survives in both private and institutional ownership. His portraits are invariably hand-tinted, a practice that he popularized, if not pioneered, in Japan – skilled native artists were employed expressly for this purpose (though colouring of photographs had been tried before in the West, it never became popular). Beato's landscape work was not generally coloured, although this became automatic with later 19th-century photographers in Japan – as is evident from the photographs in this book. His style is often described as documentary in feel – not surprising, perhaps, given his war-photography background. His work is certainly very matter-of-fact, natural and usually non-interpretive. His portrait studies of 'occupational types' seem purely observational and never condescending. A master photographer, and a hard act to follow.

Portrait of Felice Beato,
CIRCA 1864

In August 1869 Wilhelm Burger, an extremely talented Austrian photographer, arrived in Nagasaki with his 15-year-old assistant and countryman, Michael Moser. Burger was in Japan as part of an official Austrian trade and diplomatic mission to the Far East. While in Japan he took some exceptionally fine photographs, using the Nagasaki and Yokohama studios of Hikoma Ueno and Renjo Shimooka respectively. Burger left Japan in March 1870 but his young assistant, Moser, stayed on for another seven years, becoming a noted photographer and interpreter. He actually took many of the photographs which appeared in the magazine *The Far East* which started in Yokohama in 1870 and continued until 1878. It employed actual mounted photographs. Copies of the magazine are now extremely rare (19).

Another Austrian, Baron Raimund von Stillfried und Ratenitz is, after Beato, the most celebrated Western photographer of 19th-century Japan. He is also the author of at least half of the photos from the Grigoryev collection, illustrated in this book. Von Stillfried was active as a photographer in Japan from 1871–1883 and more will be said of him later.

The last significant Western photographer in 19th-century Japan was the American-Italian, Adolpho Farsari. Farsari was in the Italian Army in 1859 and left in 1863, at the age of 22, to emigrate to the United States. On arrival he joined the Union Army and fought in the Civil War until 1865. He had married a Mary Patchen, in 1863, with whom he had two children. But the family fell apart and he moved to Japan in 1873.

By 1878 he is registered as the manager of the Yokohama Cigar Co., and in 1879 had formed the partnership Sargent, Farsari & Co., trading in cigarettes and stationery. In 1881 he had bought a house and was in book-importing. Two years later, at the age of 42, he taught himself photography and shortly afterwards acquired from von Stillfried the photo studio of the Japan Photographic Association. Beato had sold his stock and negatives to von Stillfried in 1877 and it is noticeable that both Beato's and von Stillfried's negatives occasionally appear in Farsari albums. In February 1886 a fire destroyed all of his negatives and he spent the next five months travelling in Japan, rebuilding his stock.

Farsari had a daughter by his Japanese mistress and when he returned to Italy for good, in 1890, the child accompanied him. He died in 1898 but the firm in Japan continued under his name until at least 1917 (21).

Farsari's style is hard to read. More research on and comparisons of his work pre- and post-1886 are required. We know he used Beato's and von Stillfried's negatives and he may have used the works of other artists in addition. What is clear is that he employed wonderful artists since the colouring of his photographs is usually exceptional. Farsari was the last important Western photographer in 19th-century Japan and by the time he left in 1890 Japanese photographers had a complete monopoly. (I am indebted to Fred Sharf for much of the above information on Farsari.)

JAPANESE PHOTOGRAPHERS IN JAPAN

The first professional Japanese photographers in Japan were Hikoma Ueno and Renjo Shimooka who both opened studios in 1862, in Nagasaki and Yokohama respectively.

Portrait of Hikoma Ueno,
CIRCA 1864 (PHOTOGRAPHER
UNKNOWN)

Nagasaki-born Hikoma Ueno was the son of the wealthy merchant Shinnojo Ueno, who had imported the first camera into Japan. The younger Ueno was born in 1838 and studied Chinese classics from the age of 16. After graduation he enrolled at the Dutch medical school in Nagasaki and studied chemistry under Pompe Van Meedervoort. The Dutchman also conducted photographic experiments, but with limited success (1, 23).

Ueno, in his 1862 book (23), mentions studying photography under the Frenchman, Rossier. At first, Ueno's studio was not particularly successful. Not many Japanese could afford to have their photographs taken and those who could suffered from the general Japanese superstition of the time that ill-health or death would result from being photographed. Ueno had to rely, therefore, on foreign clientele until 1867. At this time of revolution in Japan, many soldiers thought they might die in battle and wanted to have their images preserved for their families. Ueno thereby prospered from this time onwards and his studio thrived until his death in 1904.

Probably because Renjo Shimooka retired from photography in 1877 Ueno's images, although rare, have survived in greater numbers. Shimooka would have missed the great tourist boom of the 1880s and 1890s when many Ueno albums and individual images were taken back to the West and preserved. (The high humidity of the Japanese climate, frequent natural disasters and the Second World War have all made the preservation of photographs in Japan extremely difficult.) Ueno was a major influence on Japanese photography and he produced technically competent work together with many important historical portraits of famous Japanese figures.

Renjo Shimooka (1823–1914) was born in Shimoda, and initially pursued his first love, painting. He switched to photography after learning the rudiments from Henry

Heusken, in Shimoda as secretary to US Consul Townsend Harris. More formal instruction was received from an American photographer in Yokohama, known as Wanshim *(sic)*, but who is as yet unidentified (24). Shimooka opened his Yokohama studio in 1862 and relied, almost exclusively, on foreign clientele. In any case he was very successful until his attempts to diversify his business interests, from 1877 onwards, led him to bankruptcy and he seems not to have escaped financial difficulties until his death in 1914.

Very little Shimooka material has so far been identified and an appraisal of his work is not yet possible. This is very disappointing, considering his reputation. I have only seen around 20–30 pieces of his work and these are all *carte-de-visite* format. There must still be many examples of his larger format work in existence and it is hoped that they will be identified before too long.

Shusaburo Usui was born in Shimoda (24) also, at an unknown date. There are different versions concerning the early period of Usui's career, but one thing certain is that he was first introduced to photography by Shimooka. Photo-historian Fukutaro Maeda suggests that Usui was taught by Shimooka during periods when he frequently returned to Shimoda from his base in Yokohama during the years 1865–68. Another historian, Sadao Umemoto, wrote that Shimooka's first wife named Mitsume was Usui's sister. Shimooka took Usui under his apprenticeship teaching him photography in the early 1860s. Then sometime between the years 1865–1868 Usui opened his first studio in Yokohama, an outdoor *shajō* (verandah). But this second version seems a bit premature for Usui first opening a studio.

A third version by the Yokohama Archives of History suggests that Usui was first introduced to photography by Shimooka but due to Shimooka's travels between Shimoda and Yokohama he was unable to fully teach Usui the craft. In order to deepen his knowledge Usui went to Yokohama and from December 1876–March 1877 he studied with the foreign photographer John Douglas who, shortly after teaching Usui, joined the Japan Photographic Association. It was around this time that Usui was thought to have set up his first studio in Yokohama.

By 1880 Usui was firmly established and ran a 'modest' advertisement in the 1880 Japan Directory that read:

Usui Artist. Corner of Ohtemachi, near the Kencho.

The best and cheapest photographer in Japan. Excellent photographs produced. Always on hand. Views of the principal places in Japan including: Tokyo, Kioto, Kobe, Nikko, Hakone, etc., etc. Albums made up with the choicest pictures on the shortest notice.

Prices fifty percent cheaper than those of any other photographer in Japan.

David Welsh, agent for Usui January 1880

As stated in this advertisement Usui was represented by agent David Welsh who also handled von Stillfried's firm — the Japan Photographic Association. This later led to a partnership between Usui and Welsh and in 1884 they set up business at no. 16 called the Yokohama Photographic Company. This was next door to von Stillfried's studio at no. 17 (formerly Beato & Co.).

This soon led to fierce competition between the two studios and it is likely that Usui's pricing policy put the von Stillfried studio out of business. In fact von Stillfried had already left Japan when the studio was sold in 1885 to Farsari & Co.

Despite Usui's extreme commerciality, he was a talented photographer who produced fine albums of photographs with artistic views and delicate hand-colouring. It is not exactly known what happened to Usui, but he is thought to have sold his studio to Farsari & Co. which occupied Usui's address at no. 16 from 1888. (I am indebted to Torin Boyd and Naomi Izakura for carrying out the above research on Usui.)

Kuichi Uchida (1844–75) did not live long enough for a full appreciation of his work to take place. Very little is known about his early life or the cause of his death. Only a handful of images have so far been attributed to him although it is not too difficult to find *carte-de-visite* photographs with his studio stamp on the reverse. In fact, the props and studio backgrounds shown in these are likely to be the key to attributing his larger format pictures.

Uchida came, at the age of 13, under the guardianship of Ryojun Matsumoto who was studying photography under Van Meedervoort. It is quite probable, therefore, that he was introduced to the art in this way and may himself have studied at the school with Hikoma Ueno and others. Anyway, it is known that at the early age of 16 he purchased photographic equipment at an auction held by the Dutch residents of Dejima. By 1865 he had opened a photo studio in Osaka with the help of Matsumoto and a year later he moved his business to Tokyo. In 1868 he opened a second studio in Yokohama. He is especially famous for taking, in 1871, photographs of the Emperor and Empress Meiji. But, generally speaking, his work, like Shimooka's, is largely unknown (1, 24, 25).

Kimbei Kusakabe (1841–1934) is an interesting and under-appreciated artist. Although little is known of his personal life, it is relatively easy to find his work today. This is because he was very successful in selling his photo albums to foreign tourists and his studio adverts can be readily seen in contemporary guide-books. In these he used his first name Kimbei (pronounced Kimbay) since this was presumably easier for foreigners to pronounce.

The photo-historian Sadao Umemoto of the Japan Photographic Association said that Kusakabe was born in Kofu, Yamanashi Prefecture. His family had a textile business and at the age of 15 or 16 he moved to Yokohama and became an apprentice of Beato, and accompanied him on a trip to Shanghai in 1867. Other more recent commentators have held that he was rather an apprentice to von Stillfried. It is of course quite possible that he was apprenticed to Beato and then worked with von Stillfried when the latter bought Beato's studio in 1877.

Anyway, by 1881 Kusakabe had his own studio in Yokohama, and in 1885 he purchased a portion of von Stillfried's stock. His subsequent albums can be seen to contain both Beato and von Stillfried pictures. Clearly he was influenced by the work of these two artists and while he seems to capture in his portrait work the essence of Beato's simple, direct and observational style his subjects seem a little more relaxed, and at ease in front of the camera. He also seems, like von Stillfried, to bring out his subjects' personalities rather more than Beato did. Being Japanese himself, this may have been easier. Kusakabe also had to be influenced by the work of Ueno and

Shimooka and he seems to me to complete the maturing process of 19th-century Japanese photography (25).

Other prolific artists were Kosaburo Tamamura (1850–?), a contemporary of Kusakabe's and Farsari's and who seems to have produced more tourist albums than any other photographer, and Isshin Ogawa (1860–1929) who concentrated on producing collotype photographic books, rather than conventional albums of albumen photographs. (Note that Ogawa is usually recorded as Kazumasa Ogawa.)

Finally, it would be wrong not to mention the following artists – examples of whose excellent work one can still occasionally come across today: Kokichi Kizu (1830–93), Hokkaidō; Matsusaburo Yokoyama, Yokohama; Reiji Esaki (1845–1909), Tokyo; Shinichi Suzuki (1835–1918), Tokyo and Yokohama; Seibei Kajima; I. Isawa, Tokyo; Matsuchi Nakajima, Tokyo; Ryo-Un-Do, Kobe; Shin-E-Do, Kobe; Sashichi Ogawa, Yokohama; R. Okamoto, Tokyo.

BARON RAIMUND VON STILLFRIED UND RATENITZ (1839–1911)

Many of the photographs in this book were taken by Baron von Stillfried, an Austrian nobleman, during the 1870s. There is not a great deal of information available on von Stillfried's life but he seems to have left the Austrian Army in 1863 and travelled to Japan where he became proficient in the language. It is unclear how long he stayed and he next crops up as an officer in Emperor Maximilian's Army in Mexico. He returned to Austria in 1867 and tried very hard to be included in the 'Imperial Austrian Expedition' to the Far East. It seems that he was not successful in being accepted officially but we know that he travelled to Japan again and arrived in July 1868, 13 months before the expedition. Upon arrival he succeeded in getting a job as an interpreter to the Prussian merchant firm of Textor & Co., in Yokohama (20, 27–29).

In 1872 an advertisement in the Yokohama *Hong List & Directory* mentions the photo studio of Stillfried & Co. But it is not clear exactly when von Stillfried took up photography. We know that he was a talented water-colourist and had studied formerly under the landscape painter Bernhard Fielder in Trieste and this artistic talent is very apparent in many of the superb photographs included in this book.

Von Stillfried had a number of studio names: The Yokohama Library, The Japan Photographic Association, and Stillfried & Andersen. It was with his partner, H. Andersen, that he bought the studio negatives and archives of Felice Beato in 1877. This explains why some of the images in this book can be recognized as coming from original Beato negatives.

Von Stillfried returned to Austria in 1883 (20) after selling his stock to Farsari & Co. A number of negatives must have ended up with Kusakabe since prints from these appear in the latter's albums with some regularity. The date of the sale of von Stillfried's stock is unclear but most sources show this as 1885. It is quite possible, therefore, that the sale took place after von Stillfried's return to Austria where he died in 1911.

Very little else is known about von Stillfried's life although I did discover a brief contemporary reference to him in an unpublished diary (30). The author was Mrs Alice Mary Rea, an amateur artist, who was on a world tour with her husband. An entry for December 1881 reads ' . . . We bought some costume photos at Baron Stillfried's – an Austrian who had lost his fortune at Monaco and came here to retrieve it. He has a large staff of Japanese artists under him, who colour most beautifully . . . '

When von Stillfried bought Beato's negatives in 1877 he continued, not unnaturally, to produce prints from them for sale. At around this time it became mandatory to register photographs with the authorities and, presumably, to number them since it is very rare to find a photograph of this period without a number. In fact its absence is often evidence that the image has been cropped. Von Stillfried numbered Beato's negatives, and his own, by scratching or painting them and his discreet form of numbering is quite distinctive.

There is a clear difference in style which is quite noticeable when comparing the

PHOTOGRAPHIC VIEWS
OF
JAPANESE SCENERY
AND ALL CLASSES OF
JAPANESE SOCIETY.
Messrs. STILLFRIED & Co.,
No. 61, Main Street, Yokohama,
beg to announce that their ALBUMS are always open for Public Inspection. Pictures of figures or views may be had either in books or singly—mounted or unmounted.
New Pictures are being added every day.
The Studio is always open during the ordinary business hours for
PORTRAITS
Large, Cabinet, or Carte de Visite size.

Von Stillfried's studio advertisement from the 1870s

work of these two great artists – Henry Rosin has done some worthwhile research on this (29).

When Beato first came to Japan in 1863 it was still a 'feudal' society, as Hugh Cortazzi describes earlier. This, plus Beato's preference for a somewhat documentary and naturalistic style of photography, meant that his images have a quite different feel from von Stillfried's later work. Von Stillfried's portraits of 'occupational types' from the 1870s, whilst technically superb, look somewhat more posed and stilted than Beato's. Certainly von Stillfried used more models than Beato, but this was because 'authentic' artisans were disappearing at a tremendous rate due to the breathtaking speed of Japan's modernization after 1868. But perhaps the main reason for the different feel of these two artists is that Beato's negatives were mainly produced in 1867–68 (a fire in 1866 destroyed his previous stock) and 10 years during that particular period of rapid change in Japan, was a very long time indeed.

This juxtapositioning in von Stillfried's 1870s albums of both his own, and Beato's work, has of course invited direct comparison and detracted, unfairly I believe, from von Stillfried's reputation as a great photographer. Their styles were indeed different, but von Stillfried, with his formal artistic training, was able often to produce more visually appealing work; many examples exist in this book. His photographs also demonstrate his ability to draw out of his subjects their characters and personalities.

I believe that this book contains the largest number of von Stillfried photographs ever published. Many of them also appear for the first time. It is to be hoped that von Stillfried will, in due course, emerge from the shadow of Felice Beato. Recognition of his photographic genius is long overdue.

THE PHOTOGRAPHS

Someone with a little knowledge of early Japanese photography could be forgiven for thinking, on first sight of the images in this book, that the photographs were all taken by Baron von Stillfried. In fact, there are at least two other photographers represented – Felice Beato and Shusaburo Usui.

The Beato images which appear here have been printed by von Stillfried from the original negatives purchased in 1877. Von Stillfried's numbering of these photographs shows that they were printed, in most cases, 10 years after the original negative was made. Nevertheless, the quality is still very good although I suspect that Grigoryev was quite selective when making his choice of photographs for his collection.

Usui's work is often confused with von Stillfried's and care has to be taken in distinguishing one from the other. I cannot recall seeing Usui's photographs being attributed and illustrated elsewhere, although his work is not exceptionally rare.

Turning now to the unidentified photographs it should be said that some controversy exists over their attribution. Worswick calls them the *shajō* group since most of them have been taken on an outside Japanese raised platform or verandah (*shajō*). Whilst there is general consensus that they are the work of one artist, there is certainly no consensus as to who this artist might be. The candidates to date have been Shimooka, Uchida and von Stillfried.

Clark Worswick, who has done more than anyone in promoting the study of Japanese photographic history, believes that the photographer is Uchida. In a fascinating article in *Image* magazine (26) he argues in favour of Japanese authorship because of the requirement for ' . . . a detailed knowledge of Japanese folk customs far beyond the command of Europeans . . .'. He also rightly points out that whilst these images appear to date from the early to mid–1870s, they do seem to suddenly disappear from the scene by the end of the 1870s and that this coincides with the early death of Uchida. He also believes that the Japanese numbering suggests a Japanese photographer with both Western and Japanese clientele.

Henry Rosin, an expert on von Stillfried, is of the opinion that this photographer is the author and has pointed out that a number of prints from the same series appeared in *The Far East*, to which von Stillfried is known to have contributed. He believes the numbering on the face of the images is similar to von Stillfried's more standard stock.

Whenever I have seen any *shajō* collections, as I have on three separate occasions, they have been grouped with known von Stillfried photographs. To me, therefore, there must have been some connection, though I am unsure precisely what it is. The arrangement of the pictures does indeed necessitate detailed knowledge of Japanese rural life, but von Stillfried could have used a consultant or assistants for this.

Personally, however, I am inclined towards Japanese authorship because these photographs have a certain 'native feel' and the scenes seem cluttered and busy compared with von Stillfried's usual rather sedate and measured style. I also believe that he did not use Japanese numbering or titles on his prints.

I am not convinced that Uchida is the photographer, however. The disappearance from circulation of the *shajō* pictures could simply have been due to any one of the numerous fires or natural disasters which were (and in the case of the latter still are) common in Japan. Another strong possibility is that they had simply become unfashionable by the 1880s. Certainly they would have seemed to depict Japan's past, rather than its present, so perhaps they didn't appeal as much as the more 'modern', beautifully coloured photographs that were appearing in strikingly elegant lacquer-covered photo-albums.

Attribution has been further complicated by a discovery recently made by the archivists of this collection at the Russian Geographical Society, St Petersburg. On the reverse of the first photograph from the *shajō* group, in Grigoryev's handwriting, is the inscription 'photograph by Luca Sudzuki'. They conjecture that the Japanese photographer concerned was therefore a Christian (Luca being, perhaps, a version of the Christian name Luke), but have not been able to discover any further information about this photographer.

His surname, more usually romanized as 'Suzuki' is, unfortunately, probably the most common of Japanese names. Still, there is a good possibility that the photographer is Shinichi Suzuki, an artist thought to have been an apprentice to Renjo Shimooka during the years 1870–76, after which he set up his own studio in Nagoya and continued to be active through the 1880s.

Circumstantially the evidence is strong. Being a Christian in Japan in the 1870s was certainly not socially acceptable and was officially discouraged. Renjo Shimooka himself was converted to Christianity in the early 1870s, which may well have influenced his apprentice, Suzuki. This style of the *shajō* pictures, as mentioned earlier, is not too dissimilar to a number of Shimooka's known *carte-de-visite* images. The props look similar, also. Suzuki could not have failed to exhibit some traces of Shimooka's style.

Publication of some of the *shajō* pictures in the Far East and the probable connection, in some way or other, with von Stillfried give the impression of a photographer comfortable moving in Western circles in Yokohama and, probably, with some knowledge of English. Shinichi Suzuki did in fact study painting with the English artist Charles Wirgman and spent some time in San Francisco, returning to Japan in 1881. He was clearly a man with an international outlook. Shinichi Suzuki must therefore now be considered a front-runner for attribution as photographer to the *shajō* series. More research needs to be done in this area, and the publication here of a relatively large number of *shajō* pictures should help in this regard.

In the photographs he selected, Grigoryev succeeded in taking back to Russia a very balanced and representative view of Japan at that time and of its recent past. Japan was moving fast, and would never be the same again.

PHOTOGRAPHIC TERMS

Daguerreotype: The first successful commercial photographic process and the one used by Eliphalet Brown in Japan in 1853–54. It was invented by Louis Daguerre in 1839. The daguerreotype is a direct positive using a sensitized copper plate which was exposed for approximately 15 minutes. The daguerrreotype is a unique photograph since no negative is used.

Wet collodion or Wet-plate process. Invented by Fredreick Scott Archer in 1851, the process involved coating a glass plate with a special chemical mixture and exposing it while still wet. Exposure would take just a few seconds but the whole operation was messy and cumbersome.

Albumen print. This refers to the very popular form of photographic printing paper introduced in 1850. It was called albumen due to its principal binding ingredient being egg-white. The vast majority of 19th-century Japanese photographs were printed on albumen.

Dry-plate process. A revolutionary development in photography and introduced in 1873. It replaced the wet collodion solution by a gelatin which, when used as the emulsion, made the transportation and storage of pre-prepared glass plates infinitely easier.

Carte de visite. CDVs were a very popular form of visiting card in the 1860s and the image size was invariably 9 x 6.5 cm. They were mounted on slightly larger card and were also used in Japan to depict portraits and views.

Collotype. A high-quality fine-grain printing process whereby gelatine is applied to a glass plate which is allowed to dry and then exposed to a photographic image. It was invented by Poitevin in 1855 and was popularized in Japan by Ogawa in the 1890s, who produced many beautiful collotype works.

Stereoscopic print: In this process, invented by Wheatstone in 1838, two photographs are taken of the same object but from slightly different angles. When both images are mounted side by side on stiff card and viewed through a stereoscopic (binocular device) an illusion of a three-dimensional view is created.

Hand-colouring of photographs. This never really became popular in Europe, where it was first introduced, but from the 1870s onwards, in Japan, it was invariably the practice to colour both views and portraits. It may be that Beato was the first to employ it consistently in Japan. Many examples of water-colouring by Japanese artists show exquisite taste and outstanding skill.

BIBLIOGRAPHY

1. Ozawa, Takesi. 'The history of early photography in Japan.' *History of Photography*, vol 5, no 4, October 1981. See also Bennett, T. B. 'The early photographers, Photographing Japan 1860s–1890s.' Four-part article, *Japan Digest*, Jan, Apr, Jul, Oct 1991.

2. Hawks, F. L. *Narrative of the expedition of an American Squadron to the China Seas and Japan, performed in the years 1852, 1853 and 1854.* Washington, 1856.

3. 'Through Japan with a Camera.' *Photographic News'* October 1859–February 1860.

4. Himeno, J. *The Japanese modernisation and international informativeness viewed from old photographs.* Old Photography Study 1, University of Nagasaki, 1994 (unpublished, in Japanese).

5. Jocelyn, The Hon. W. N., China and Japan 1858–1859. Private Journal.

6. Rogers, G. W. 'Early recollections of Yokohama 1859–1864.' *The Japan Weekly Mail,* 5 December 1903.

7. Notehelfer, F. G. *Japan Through American Eyes: The Journal of Francis Hall, Kanagawa and Yokohama 1859–1866.* Princeton University Press, 1992.

8. Westfield, T. C. *The Japanese, Their Manners and Their Customs.* Photographic News Office, London, 1862.

9. Saitoh T. F. 'Looking at the origins of the history of photographs – miscellaneous data stories.' *Yokohama Kaiko Shiyokan Kanjo News,* 3 May 1990 (in Japanese).

10. Negretti, P. A. 'Henry Negretti – gentleman and photographic pioneer.' *The Photographic Collector,* vol 5 no 1 1984

11. Saitoh, Takio. 'Photography in Yokohama and W. Saunders.' *The Photo Historian,* no 86, autumn 1989.

12. Advertisments for Charles Parker's studio in the *Japan Herald,* September 1863; 30 May 1864; 22 July 1865.

13. First mention of Felice Beato: *Illustrated London News,* 13 July 1863.

14. Clark, John. *A Chronology of Felix (Felice) Beato.* Privately printed (Fraser and Osman) 1989.

15. *Yokohama Mainichi.* Newspaper article on Beato, 5 December 1884 (in Japanese).

16. Woods, Sir H. F. *Spunyarn, Strands from a Sailor's Life.* Hutchinson & Co., London, 1924.

17. Saitoh, Takio. *F. Beato Bakumatsu Nihon Shashinshu.* Yokohama Archives of History, 1987 (in Japanese).

18. Phillip, Seigert et al. *Felice Beato in Japan.* Edition Braus, Heidelberg, 1991.

19. White, Stephen. 'The Far East.' *Image* 34, nos 1–2, 1991.

20. Rosenberg, G. *Wilhelm Burger.* Brandstatter Vienna/Munich 1984.

21. *Keelings Guide to Japan,* 4th edition, 1890.

22. Ueno, I. *Shiyashin no Kaiso, Ueno Hikoma.* Sangyo Noritsu Tanki Daigaku, 1975 (in Japanese).

23. Ueno and Horie. *Introduction to Science.* 1862 (in Japanese)

24. Bennett, T. B. *Early Japanese Images.* C. Tuttle & Co, Tokyo, 1995.

25. Yokohama Kaiko Shiryokan (ed) *Meiji No Nihon.* Yokohama Shashin No Sekai, Yokohama 1990 (in Japanese).

26. Worswick, C. 'The Disappearance of Uchida, Kyuichi and the Discovery Nineteenth Century Asian Photography.' *Image,* vol. 36, nos 1–2, Spring-Summer 1993.

27. Winkel, Margarita. *Souvenirs from Japan.* Bamboo Publishing Ltd, London, 1991.

28. Edel, Chantal (trans). *Once Upon a Time. Visions of Old Japan from the Photos of Beato and Stillfried and the words of Pierre Loti.* Friendly Press Inc, New York, 1986.

29. Rosin, Henry. 'Etudes sur les debuts de la photographie japonaise au 19e siécle.' *Bulletin Association Franco-Japonaise,* no. 16 (April). 1987 (pp. 33–39).

30. Rea, Mary Alice. Private journal, 1881.

The Treaty Ports:
Yokohama and Hakodate

YOKOHAMA, MAIN STR. 418

1. *Yokohama – main street in the foreign quarter.*

PHOTOGRAPHER VON STILLFRIED

2. *Yokohama – Takashimacho.*
PHOTOGRAPHER VON STILLFRIED

3. *Yokohama – Water Street.*
PHOTOGRAPHER VON STILLFRIED

4. *Yokohama – a bird's-eye view.*
PHOTOGRAPHER UNKNOWN

5. Kanasawa, near Yokohama

6. *Kanasawa – waterfront.*
PHOTOGRAPHER POSSIBLY USUI OR SUZUKI

7. *Kanasawa – near Yokohama.*
PHOTOGRAPHER BEATO

8. *Junk off the coast.*
PHOTOGRAPHER UNKNOWN

9. *Ferry boat.* PHOTOGRAPHER BEATO

10. PHOTOGRAPHER BEATO

TOKAIDO.

11. *On the Tōkaidō.*
PHOTOGRAPHER BEATO

12. *Japanese shop.*

13. *Japanese shop.*
PHOTOGRAPHER VON STILLFRIED

14. *Japanese shop.*
PHOTOGRAPHER VON STILLFRIED

15. *Japanese curio shop.*

PHOTOGRAPHER VON STILLFRIED

16. *Garden of a private house (dog lying on the verandah).*
PHOTOGRAPHER BEATO

HAKODADI.

17. *Part of Hakodate. Below the woods to the right is the Russian Orthodox church.*

PHOTOGRAPHER VON STILLFRIED

18. *Japanese inn on the outskirts of Hakodate.*

PHOTOGRAPHER VON STILLFRIED

19. *The volcano Romanotaki near Hakodate and a mountain lake.*
PHOTOGRAPHER PROBABLY USUI

20. *The same volcano and lake from the other side.*

21. *View of the shore of Hokkaidō with an Ainu sitting on a stone.*
PHOTOGRAPHER VON STILLFRIED

Street Life

22. *A porter.*

PHOTOGRAPHER BEATO

23. *A pedlar.*

PHOTOGRAPHER BEATO

24. *A group of porters.*
PHOTOGRAPHER UNKNOWN

25. *A travelling seller of 'amazake' (a sweet drink made from fermented rice, mildly alcoholic and usually served warm).*
PHOTOGRAPHER BEATO

26. *A portable stand, advertising 'shiruko' (a sweet thick liquid made from beans) with a rickshaw man and his passenger on the left.*
PHOTOGRAPHER VON STILLFRIED

27. *Pushing a heavy load.*
PHOTOGRAPHER VON STILLFRIED

28. *'Kago', a form of litter used e.g when travelling in the mountains.*
PHOTOGRAPHER BEATO

29. *'Norimono', an elaborate form of 'kago' or palanquin, used by daimyō and senior officials.*
PHOTOGRAPHER VON STILLFRIED

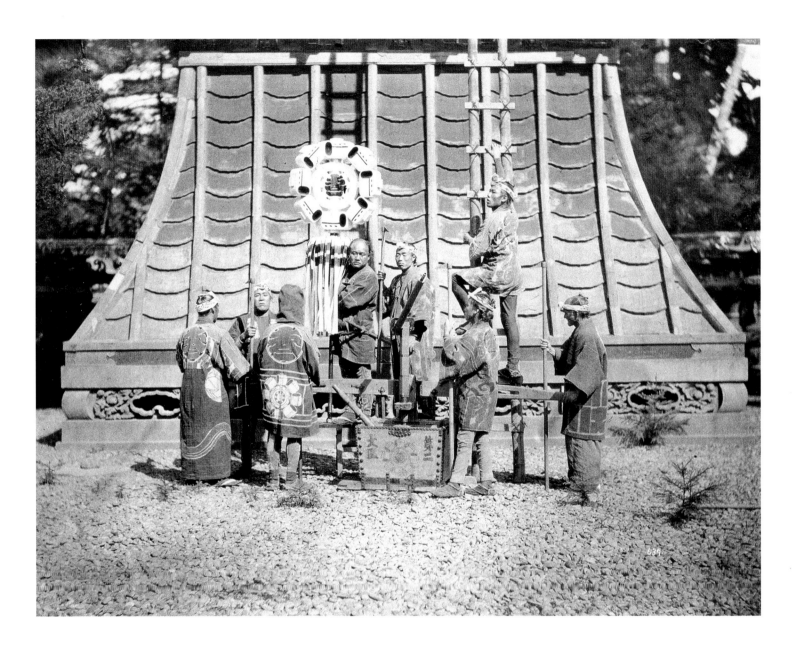

30. *Firemen.*
PHOTOGRAPHER VON STILLFRIED

31. *A beggar with samisen and child.*
PHOTOGRAPHER VON STILLFRIED

32. *Cripples begging.*
PHOTOGRAPHER VON STILLFRIED

Domestic Life

33. *Lady bowing to a samurai.*
PHOTOGRAPHER UNKNOWN

34. *Greeting a guest.*
PHOTOGRAPHER UNKNOWN

35. *Woman resting with her head on a wooden pillow.*
PHOTOGRAPHER VON STILLFRIED

36. *Man having a bath.*
PHOTOGRAPHER POSSIBLY SUZUKI

37. *Woman having her hair put up.*
PHOTOGRAPHER VON STILLFRIED

38. *Woman tidying herself up, holding a metal-cased mirror, with a hibachi (charcoal burner), and a toilet table.*
PHOTOGRAPHER VON STILLFRIED

39. *Japanese breakfast.*
PHOTOGRAPHER VON STILLFRIED

40. *Family meal on verandah.*
PHOTOGRAPHER POSSIBLY SUZUKI

41. *Family meal on verandah, man on the right being offered a titbit.*
PHOTOGRAPHER POSSIBLY SUZUKI

42. *Man drinking tea served by a woman. Woman on left smoking a Japanese pipe (kiseru).*

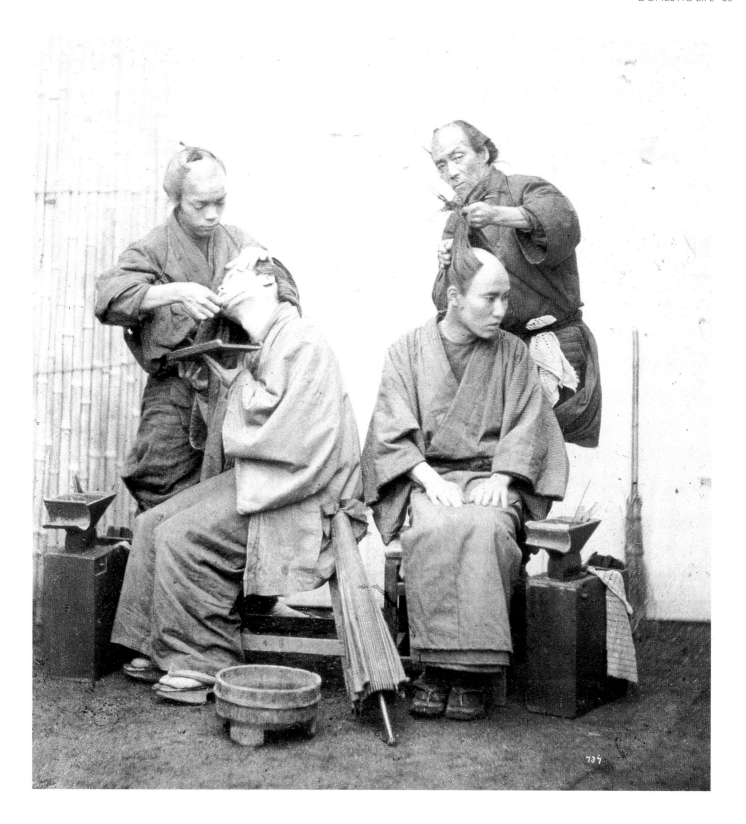

43. *Man on the left being shaved, man on the right having his topknot prepared.*

PHOTOGRAPHER VON STILLFRIED

44. *Old man and two women, kettle on the charcoal burner (hibachi) with Japanese-style teapot and cups.*
PHOTOGRAPHER VON STILLFRIED

45. *Playing 'go' (Japanese chequers).*
PHOTOGRAPHER VON STILLFRIED

46. *Traditional New Year amusements, playing battledore and shuttlecock and flying kites. In the background is part of a New Year decoration.*

PHOTOGRAPHER UNKNOWN

47. *Ladies with traditional New Year ornaments of straw and New Year foods.*
PHOTOGRAPHER UNKNOWN

48. *Paying a visit at New Year. The house has traditional New Year decorations.*
PHOTOGRAPHER POSSIBLY SUZUKI

49. *Celebrating the girls or dolls festival on the third of the third month.*
PHOTOGRAPHER POSSIBLY SUZUKI

50. *Celebration of a Buddhist festival.*
PHOTOGRAPHER POSSIBLY SUZUKI

51. *At a festival. Women playing drums at the left.*
PHOTOGRAPHER POSSIBLY SUZUKI

52. *Lady playing the samisen.*
PHOTOGRAPHER VON STILLFRIED

53. *Lady playing the koto, a form of Japanese harp.*
PHOTOGRAPHER VON STILLFRIED

54. *Lady dancing.*
PHOTOGRAPHER BEATO

55. *Two men practising archery.*

56. *Archery practice.*

Costumes and
Portraits

57. *Warrior in traditional armour.*
PHOTOGRAPHER UNKNOWN

58. *Two men dressed as samurai carrying two swords.*
PHOTOGRAPHER VON STILLFRIED

59. *Man wearing court costume with court headgear (kammuri).*

PHOTOGRAPHER VON STILLFRIED

60. *The same man as shown in photograph 59, in a different pose.*

PHOTOGRAPHER VON STILLFRIED

61. *Man wearing traditional haori and hakama and formal headgear (eboshi).*

PHOTOGRAPHER UNKNOWN

62. *Man wearing traditional haori and hakama and formal headgear (eboshi).*
PHOTOGRAPHER VON STILLFRIED

63. *Man wearing formal dress (possibly a mixture of styles for the photograph) and headgear (eboshi).*
PHOTOGRAPHER VON STILLFRIED

64. *Actor dancing wearing a mask in a performance of kyogen, a comic interlude in a Noh performance (Noh are traditional classic dramas in verse).*
PHOTOGRAPHER VON STILLFRIED

65. *Actor wearing mask in a Noh performance.*

66. *Portrait of the Japanese artist who coloured most of the photographs in this collection.*
PHOTOGRAPHER VON STILLFRIED

67. *O-Kin san, the owner of the tavern 'on the 101st step in Yokohama'.*

PHOTOGRAPHER VON STILLFRIED

68. *Japanese lady showing traditional dress and hair style.*

69. *Portrait of an old woman.*

PHOTOGRAPHER VON STILLFRIED

70. *Portrait of a man.*

PHOTOGRAPHER VON STILLFRIED

71. *Portrait of a man.*
PHOTOGRAPHER VON STILLFRIED

72. *Old man informally dressed holding a fan on which the characters inscribed (from left) mean 'old man, long life, and great Japan'.*

PHOTOGRAPHER VON STILLFRIED

73. *An itinerant dentist. The box, containing his instruments, bears the Chinese characters meaning 'everything for the inside of the honourable mouth'.*
PHOTOGRAPHER BEATO

74. *Servant girl carrying teapot and with tea cups on tray.*
PHOTOGRAPHER BEATO

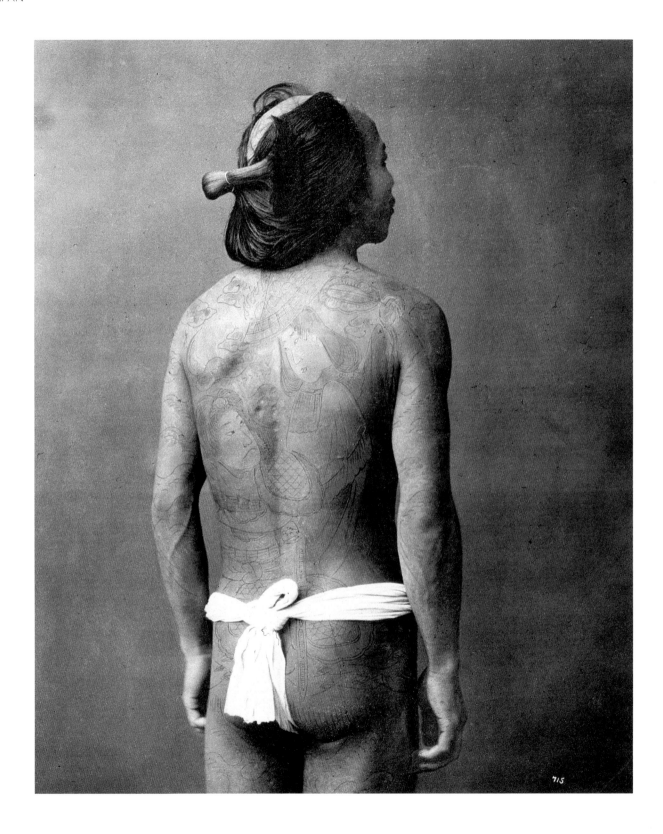

75. *Tattooed torso of man with a top knot.*

PHOTOGRAPHER VON STILLFRIED

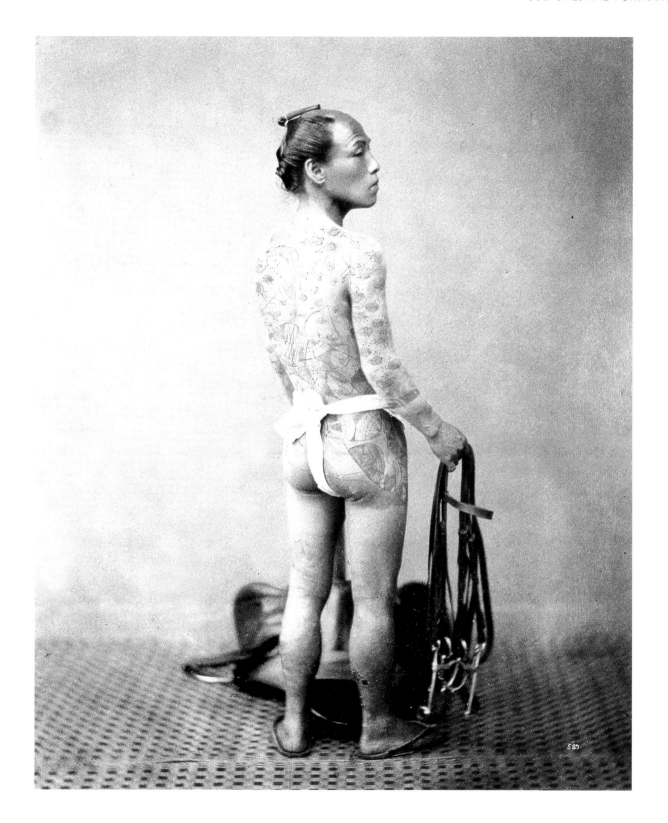

76. *A 'betto' or groom with tattooed body.*
PHOTOGRAPHER BEATO

77. *Woman wearing geta (wooden clogs) and carrying a child on her back.*

PHOTOGRAPHER BEATO

78. *Woman with children.*

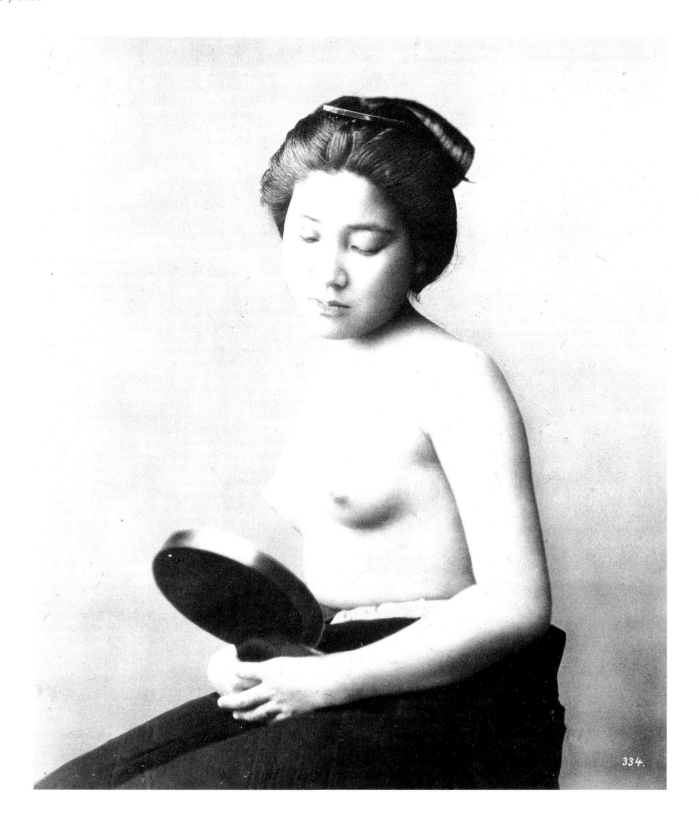

79. *A woman with her breasts uncovered, contemplating herself in a mirror.*
PHOTOGRAPHER VON STILLFRIED

80. *A woman in informal costume.*
PHOTOGRAPHER VON STILLFRIED

81. *A woman with a samisen.*

PHOTOGRAPHER VON STILLFRIED

82. *Portrait of a girl with traditional hair style, kimono and obi (sash).*

PHOTOGRAPHER VON STILLFRIED

83. *A high-class courtesan (Oiran) on the left in traditional costume and her attendant.*
PHOTOGRAPHER UNKNOWN

Farming and Handicrafts

84. *Ploughing.*
PHOTOGRAPHER POSSIBLY SUZUKI

85. *Manuring.*
PHOTOGRAPHER POSSIBLY SUZUKI

86. *Planting rice seedlings.*
PHOTOGRAPHER POSSIBLY SUZUKI

87. *Surrounding the sown fields with scarecrows and rattles to keep away birds.*
PHOTOGRAPHER POSSIBLY SUZUKI

88. *Harvesting.*
PHOTOGRAPHER POSSIBLY SUZUKI

89. *Harvesting.*
PHOTOGRAPHER POSSIBLY SUZUKI

90. *Threshing.*

PHOTOGRAPHER POSSIBLY SUZUKI

91. *Peeling the grain.*
PHOTOGRAPHER POSSIBLY SUZUKI

92. *Winnowing.*
PHOTOGRAPHER POSSIBLY SUZUKI

93. *Sifting.*
PHOTOGRAPHER POSSIBLY SUZUKI

94. *Pounding rice.*

PHOTOGRAPHER UNKNOWN

95. *Pestle for pounding rice.*

96. *Collecting water from a well.*

PHOTOGRAPHER VON STILLFRIED

97. *Washing rice before grinding.*
PHOTOGRAPHER UNKNOWN

98. *Hand-grinding.*
PHOTOGRAPHER POSSIBLY SUZUKI

99. *Hand-grinding.*

PHOTOGRAPHER POSSIBLY SUZUKI

100. *Spinning threads.*
PHOTOGRAPHER POSSIBLY SUZUKI

101. *Making the warp.*
PHOTOGRAPHER POSSIBLY SUZUKI

102. *Weaving.*
PHOTOGRAPHER POSSIBLY SUZUKI

103. *Making paper.*
PHOTOGRAPHER POSSIBLY SUZUKI

104. *Making umbrellas.*
PHOTOGRAPHER POSSIBLY SUZUKI

105. *Making paper lanterns.*
PHOTOGRAPHER POSSIBLY SUZUKI

Buddhist Temples and Shintō Shrines

106. *Banners announcing a festival at a shrine dedicated to Hachiman (the god of war).*

107. *Daibutsu (Great Buddha) at Kamakura.*

PHOTOGRAPHER VON STILLFRIED

108. *A temple probably in Yokohama.*

PHOTOGRAPHER UNKNOWN

109. *Temple, possibly in Nikko.*

110. *Ishiyama temple near Kyoto where Murasaki Shikibu is said to have composed parts of the Tale of Genji, the famous novel of the 11th century.*

PHOTOGRAPHER UNKNOWN

111. *Ishiyama temple. Stone lanterns.*

PHOTOGRAPHER VON STILLFRIED

112. *Yōmeimon, famous gateway to the shrine at Nikko commemorating Tokugawa Ieyasu, the first Tokugawa Shōgun.*
PHOTOGRAPHER UNKNOWN

113. *Torii (portal) in front of the shrine at Atago-yama in Tokyo.*
PHOTOGRAPHER UNKNOWN

114. *One of the portals of the Shiba temple of Zōjōji in Tokyo.*

PHOTOGRAPHER VON STILLFRIED

115. *Funeral lanterns by the ablution basin at the Shiba temple.*

PHOTOGRAPHER UNKNOWN

116. *Entrance to the grave of one of the Tokugawa family at Shiba temple.*
PHOTOGRAPHER USUI

117. *Shiba temple.*

PHOTOGRAPHER USUI

118. *Collector of donations for a temple.*

PHOTOGRAPHER VON STILLFRIED

119. *Buddhist priests or monks.*

PHOTOGRAPHER VON STILLFRIED

120. *Buddhist priest meditating.*
PHOTOGRAPHER UNKNOWN

121. *Man with an image of Daruma (Bodhidharma, the founder of the Zen sect).*

PHOTOGRAPHER UNKNOWN

122. *Carrying a 'mikoshi'*
PHOTOGRAPHER UNKNOWN